SHORT OVERTURE FOR STRINGS

by

Jean Berger

This score takes approximately 5 minutes to perform. It was written with the purpose of enlarging the repertoire of string music that—while not without challenge—could yet be played and performed by an amateur group. The emphasis is on the word "amateur". Hence all dynamic and tempo indications ought to be interpreted flexibly and should be adapted to the needs and the level of the technical proficiency of the performing ensemble.

J. B.

ISBN 0-7935-5702-X

G. SCHIRMER, *Inc.*

DISTRIBUTED BY
HAL•LEONARD® CORPORATION
7777 W. BLUEMOUND RD. P.O. BOX 13819 MILWAUKEE, WI 53213

HL50343030

to Alan Carter

SHORT OVERTURE
for Strings

Allegro, non troppo ♩= 96

Jean Berger

20
f
mp
mf
pizz.
30
p
arco

40
mf
f
mp
pizz.
arco
50
44397

div.
arco
sfz
p
60
mf
unis.
ff
fff
pizz.
meno f
arco
mf

70
Molto più mosso 𝅗𝅥 =132
pp
arco
pp
mp cantabile
sempre pp
sempre pp
arco
mp cantabile
pp
80
div.

90
unis.
pp
pp subito
mf
mf
sempre pp
div.
sempre pp
f
f
arco
f
100
pizz.

div.
110
ff
unis.
f
f
ff
mf
unis.
mf
mf
mf
f
mf
arco
mf
ff
ff
ff
ff
ff
Molto meno mosso (𝅗𝅥 = ♩)
pizz.
120
arco
PP sub.
pizz.
arco
mp
PP sub.
mp
mf
mf
mp
mf

poco a poco acce - le - ran - do al - - - - -
130
mf
mp
Tempo I°
f
140

poco rit.
a tempo
p
p
ff
ff
150
f
f
f
f
mf
mf
mp
mp
mp
160
p
p
p
f
f
pizz.
p
f

170
arco
molto ritard.
180

a tempo
p
p
p
190
p
mf
mf
mf
mf
f
f
f
f
ff
ff
ff
ff
ff
fff
fff
fff
fff
fff

Violin I

to Alan Carter

SHORT OVERTURE
for Strings

Allegro, non troppo 𝅗𝅥 = 96

Jean Berger

44397 c

40
mf
f
mp
50
1
mf
1
p
div.
60
unis.
ff
fff
pizz.
meno f
arco
mf
70
Molto più mosso 𝅗𝅥 = 132
3
mp cantabile
80
div.

90
unis
pp
100
sempre pp
div.
ff
110
unis.
mf
ff
Molto meno mosso
pizz.
pp sub.
120
1
arco
mp
3
poco a poco acce - le - ran - do al - - 130 - - -
mf
Tempo I°
f
140
poco rit.
a tempo

150
p
f
1
mp
1
p
160
f
p
f
170
ff
meno f
mf
p
molto ritard.
180
pp
a tempo
6
p
mf
190
f
ff
fff

Viola

to Alan Carter

SHORT OVERTURE
for Strings

Allegro, non troppo 𝅗𝅥 = 96

Jean Berger

44397c

mp
mf
40
f
1
pizz.
mf
50
3
arco
sfz
p
p
60
1
ff
fff
pizz.
meno f
2
70
Molto più mosso
= 132
arco
pp
sempre pp
80

90
mf
f
100
f
110
mf
Molto meno mosso (𝅗𝅥 = ♩)
ff
2
120
mf
3
poco a poco acce - le - ran - do al
mp
mf
130
Tempo I°
f
140
poco rit.
a tempo
ff
1

150
f
mf
mp
f
160
p
1
mp
f
ff
170
meno f
mf
p
molto rit.
180
a tempo
2
pp
p
mf
190
f
ff
fff

Violin II

to Alan Carter

SHORT OVERTURE
for Strings

Allegro, non troppo 𝅗𝅥 = 96

Jean Berger

4397c

40
mf
f
50
mp
mf
p
60
div.
unis.
mf
ff
fff
pizz.
meno f
arco
mf
70
Molto più mosso ♩ = 132
pp
sempre pp
80

90
pp subito
div.
100
sempre pp
unis.
f
110
mf
ff
Molto meno mosso
pizz.
pp sub.
120
1
arco
mp
3
poco a poco acce - le - ran - do
130
al
mf
Tempo I°
f
140
poco rit.
a tempo

150
p
f
1
mp
2
p
160
f
ff
170
meno f
mf
molto ritard.
180
a tempo
2
3
1
2
Va.
p
mf
190
f
ff
fff

Violin II

to Alan Carter

SHORT OVERTURE
for Strings

Allegro, non troppo 𝅗𝅥 = 96

Jean Berger

4397c

40
mf
f
50
1
mp
mf
1
p
60
1
1
div.
unis.
mf
ff
fff
pizz.
meno f
arco
mf
70
Molto più mosso 𝅗𝅥 = 132
pp
sempre pp
80

90
pp subito
div.
sempre pp
100
unis.
f
110
mf
ff
Molto meno mosso (𝅗𝅥 = ♩)
pizz.
pp sub.
120
1
arco
mp
3
mf
poco a poco acce - le - ran - do
130
al
Tempo I°
f
140
poco rit.
a tempo

150
p
f
1
mp
2
p
160
f
ff
170
meno f
mf
molto ritard.
180
a tempo
Va.
mf
190
f
ff
fff

Violin II

to Alan Carter

SHORT OVERTURE
for Strings

Allegro, non troppo 𝅗𝅥 = 96

Jean Berger

40
mf
f
mp
1
50
mf
1
p
60
1
1
div.
unis.
mf
ff
fff
pizz.
3
2
meno f
4
4
arco
70
Molto più mosso
𝅗𝅥 = 132
mf
pp
sempre pp
80

90
pp subito
div.
100
sempre pp
unis.
f
110
mf
ff
Molto meno mosso
pizz.
120
arco
pp sub.
mp
poco a poco acce - le - ran - do
130
al
mf
Tempo I°
f
140
poco rit.
a tempo

150
p
f
mp
p
160
f
ff
170
meno f
mf
molto ritard.
180
a tempo
Va.
p
mf
190
f
ff
fff

Violin II

to Alan Carter

SHORT OVERTURE
for Strings

Allegro, non troppo 𝅗𝅥 = 96

Jean Berger

44397c

40
mf
f
50
1
mp
mf
1
p
60
1
1
div.
unis.
mf
ff
fff
pizz.
meno f
arco
mf
70 Molto più mosso 𝅗𝅥 = 132
pp
sempre pp
80

90
pp subito
div.
sempre pp
100
unis.
f
110
mf
ff
Molto meno mosso
pizz.
pp sub.
120
1
arco
mp
3
poco a poco acce - le - ran - do
130
al
mf
Tempo I°
f
140
poco rit.
a tempo

150
160
170
meno f
molto ritard.
180
a tempo
Va.
190

Violin I

to Alan Carter

SHORT OVERTURE
for Strings

Allegro, non troppo ♩ = 96

Jean Berger

4397 c

40
mf
f
mp
50
1
mf
p
div.
60
unis.
ff
fff
pizz.
meno f
arco
mf
70
Molto più mosso = 132
3
mp cantabile
80
div.

90
unis
pp
sempre pp
100
div.
ff
110
unis.
mf
ff
Molto meno mosso
pizz.
pp sub.
120
1
arco
mp
3
poco a poco acce - le - ran - do al - - 130 - - - -
mf
Tempo I°
f
140
poco rit.
a tempo

150
160
170
meno f
molto ritard.
180
a tempo
190

Violin I

to Alan Carter

SHORT OVERTURE
for Strings

Allegro, non troppo 𝅗𝅥 = 96

Jean Berger

4397 c

40
mf
f
mp
50
1
mf
1
p
div.
60
unis.
ff
fff
pizz.
meno f
arco
mf
70
Molto più mosso 𝅗𝅥 = 132
3
mp cantabile
80
div.

90
unis
pp
sempre pp
100
div.
ff
110
unis.
mf
ff
Molto meno mosso
pizz.
pp sub.
120
1
arco
mp
3
poco a poco acce - le - ran - do al - - 130 - - -
mf
Tempo I°
f
140
poco rit.
a tempo

150
p
f
1
mp
1
p
160
f
p
f
170
ff
meno f
mf
p
molto ritard.
180
pp
a tempo
6
p
mf
190
f
ff
fff

Violin I

to Alan Carter

SHORT OVERTURE
for Strings

Allegro, non troppo 𝅗𝅥 = 96

Jean Berger

44397 c

40
mf
f
mp
50
mf
p
div.
60
unis.
ff
fff
pizz.
meno f
arco
mf
70
Molto più mosso
mp cantabile
80
div.

90
unis
pp
sempre pp
100
div.
ff
110
unis.
mf
ff
Molto meno mosso
pizz.
pp sub.
120
1
arco
mp
3
poco a poco acce - le - ran - do al - - 130 - - - -
mf
Tempo I°
f
140
poco rit.
a tempo

150
p
f
1
mp
1
p
160
f
p
f
170
ff
meno f
molto ritard.
180
mf
p
pp
a tempo
6
p
mf
190
f
ff
fff

Violin II

to Alan Carter

SHORT OVERTURE
for Strings

Allegro, non troppo 𝅗𝅥 = 96

Jean Berger

40
mf
f
mp
50
mf
1
p
60
div.
unis.
mf
ff
fff
pizz.
meno f
arco
mf
70
Molto più mosso 𝅗𝅥 = 132
pp
sempre pp
80

90
pp subito
div.
100
sempre pp
unis.
f
110
mf
ff
Molto meno mosso
pizz.
120
1
arco
mp
pp sub.
3
poco a poco acce - le - ran - do
130
al
mf
Tempo I°
f
140
poco rit.
a tempo

150
p
f
1
2
mp
p
160
f
ff
170
meno f
mf
molto ritard.
180
a tempo
3
Va.
mf
190
f
ff
fff

Violin I

to Alan Carter

SHORT OVERTURE
for Strings

Allegro, non troppo 𝅗𝅥 = 96

Jean Berger

4397 c

40
mf
f
mp
50
mf
p
div.
60
unis.
ff
fff
pizz.
meno f
arco
mf
70
Molto più mosso
= 132
mp cantabile
80
div.

90
unis
pp
100
sempre pp
div.
ff
110
unis.
mf
ff
Molto meno mosso
pizz.
pp sub.
120
1
arco
mp
3
poco a poco acce - le - ran - do al - - 130 - - -
mf
Tempo I°
f
140
poco rit.
a tempo

150
p
f
mp
p
160
f
p
f
170
ff
meno f
mf
p
molto ritard.
180
pp
a tempo
6
p
mf
190
f
ff
fff

Viola

to Alan Carter

SHORT OVERTURE
for Strings

Allegro, non troppo 𝅗𝅥 = 96

Jean Berger

mp
mf
40
f
1
pizz.
mf
50
3
arco
sfz
p
p
60
1
ff
fff
pizz.
meno f
70
Molto più mosso
= 132
2
arco
pp
sempre pp
80

90
mf
f
100
f
110
mf
Molto meno mosso
120
ff
2
mf
3
poco a poco acce - le - ran - do al
130
mp
mf
Tempo I°
f
140
poco rit.
a tempo
ff
1

150
160
170
meno f
molto rit.
180
a tempo
190

Viola

to Alan Carter

SHORT OVERTURE
for Strings

Allegro, non troppo 𝅗𝅥 = 96

Jean Berger

mp
mf
40
f
1
pizz.
mf
50
3
arco
sfz
p
p
60
1
ff
fff
pizz.
meno f
70
Molto più mosso
= 132
2
arco
pp
sempre pp
80

90
mf
f
100
f
110
mf
Molto meno mosso
ff
2
120
mf
3
poco a poco acce - le - ran - do al
mp
mf
130
Tempo I°
f
140
poco rit.
a tempo
ff
1

150
f
mf
mp
f
160
p
1
mp
f
ff
170
meno f
mf
p
molto rit.
180
a tempo
2
pp
p
mf
190
f
ff
fff

Cello

to Alan Carter

SHORT OVERTURE
for Strings

Allegro, non troppo 𝅗𝅥 = 96

Jean Berger

arco
p
60
1
2
ff
fff
pizz.
meno f
70
Molto più mosso
= 132
2
4
arco
mp
cantabile
80
90
mf
100
f
ff

110
2
mf
ff
Molto meno mosso
1
120
mf
1
mp
mp
poco a poco acce - le - ran - do al
mf
130
Tempo I°
f
140
poco rit.
a tempo
ff
1

150
160
170
molto ritard.
meno f
180
a tempo
190

Cello

to Alan Carter

SHORT OVERTURE
for Strings

Allegro, non troppo ♩ = 96

Jean Berger

arco
p
60
1
2
ff
fff
pizz.
meno f
70
Molto più mosso
= 132
2
4
arco
mp
cantabile
80
90
mf
f
100
ff

110
2
mf
ff
Molto meno mosso (𝅗𝅥 = ♩)
1
120
mf
1
mp
mp
poco a poco acce - le - ran - do al - - - -
130
mf
Tempo I°
f
140
poco rit.
a tempo
ff
1

150
f
mf
2
f
p
160
1
f
mp
2
ff
170
meno f
molto ritard.
2
3
mf
a tempo
180
pp
p
mf
190
f
ff
fff

Cello

to Alan Carter

SHORT OVERTURE
for Strings

Allegro, non troppo 𝅗𝅥 = 96

Jean Berger

arco
p
60
1
2
ff
pizz.
fff
meno f
70
Molto più mosso
𝅗𝅥 = 132
2
4
arco
mp
cantabile
80
90
mf
100
f
ff

110
Molto meno mosso
120
mf
ff
mf
mp
mp
poco a poco acce - le - ran - do al
130
mf
Tempo I°
f
140
poco rit.
a tempo
ff

150
f
mf
2
f
p
160
1
f
mp
2
ff
170
molto ritard.
2
3
meno f
a tempo
mf
180
pp
p
190
mf
f
ff
fff

arco
pizz.
arco
Molto meno mosso
poco a
poco acce - le - ran - do al
Tempo I°
poco rit.
a tempo
pizz.
V. I
arco
molto ritard.
a tempo
Cello

Bass

to Alan Carter

SHORT OVERTURE
for Strings

Jean Berg

44397c

90
arco
100
pizz.
arco
Molto meno mosso
120
poco a
poco acce - le - ran - do al
130
Tempo I°
140
poco rit.
a tempo
150
pizz.
160
V. I
arco
170
molto ritard.
180
a tempo
190
Cello

Bass

to Alan Carter

SHORT OVERTURE
for Strings

Allegro, non troppo 𝅗𝅥 = 96

Jean Berge

arco
pizz.
arco
Molto meno mosso
poco a
poco acce - le - ran - do al
Tempo I°
poco rit.
a tempo
pizz.
V. I
arco
molto ritard.
a tempo
Cello

Bass

to Alan Carter

SHORT OVERTURE
for Strings

Jean Berge